THE
BEST PRACTICES
OF
EXECUTIVE
COACHING

Paul J. Forti, Ph.D.

Lulu Publishing Services rev. date: 08/20/2018

CONTENTS

I started this book about five years ago but never had the time or inclination to complete it. Now, as I enter my semi-retirement period of life, I have found the time and passion to complete this book and offer my experience and whatever skills I have used in my coaching practice.

The purpose of this book is to share with Human Resource professionals some techniques and tools that may be useful for coaching. It can also be an instructional book for those thinking about coaching. It defines what coaching is and what makes for a successful coaching experience, as well as offering some details about the various tools that can be used to establish a successful coaching experience.

I hope you find this information useful.

I have enjoyed putting it together and it is my way of giving back to the coaching community for all the wonderful experiences I have had. To all the magnificent coaches and clients I have had the opportunity to work with, I say thank you.

Paul J. Forti, Ph.d.
Business Psychologist

DEFINING EXECUTIVE COACHING

Executive coaching has been generally defined as an experiential and individualized leader development process that builds a leader's capability to achieve short and long-term organizational goals. It is conducted through one-on-one interactions, driven by data from multiple perspectives and based on mutual trust and respect. The organization, an executive and the executive coach work in partnership to achieve maximum impact.

To give a better understanding of the terms, lets break down the common elements as follows:

Experiential. The development of the leader is accomplished primarily by practical, on the job approaches rather than through classroom or more abstract methods.

Individualized. The goals and specific actives are tailored to the unique aspects of the individual and the organizational system.

Leader development process. Executive coaching focuses on developing the executive's ability to influence, motivate and lead others. Rather than relying on tactical problem solving or basic skill acquisition, executive coaching develops strategic thinking skills.

Leader. A broad term used to mean any individual who has the potential of making a significant contribution to the mission and purpose of the organization;

One on One. The primary coaching activities take place between the individual leader and the coach. The goal is to build capability as a leader and develop new ways of thinking, feeling, acting, learning and relating to others which builds individual and organizational effectiveness.

Data from Multiple Perspectives. In order for the executive and his principal stakeholders to understand, clarify and commit to appropriate coaching goals, various data collection methods are used to identify key factors and skills required in the organizational context. The appropriate use of interviews and standardized instruments assures accuracy and validity of data gathered from people representing a range of perspectives within the organization.

Mutual Trust and Respect. Adult learning works best when the executive and the coach, along with other members of the organization, treat each other as equals, focus on their mutual strengths and believe in each other's integrity and commitment to both coaching and the organization.

Executive Coaching involves three levels of learning:

1. Tactical problem solving
2. Developing leadership capabilities and new ways of thinking and acting that generalize to other situations and roles
3. Learning how to learn. That is, developing skills and habits of self-reflection. This ensures that new learning will continue after coaching ends.

The third level is an important and necessary part of the coaching process. It aims to eliminate an executive's dependency on his/her coach and form habits of learning and self-reflection that will last a lifetime, enabling him to keep developing throughout his career.

The Coaching Partnership

The coaching partnership is a win-win approach in which all partners plan the process together, communicate openly, and work cooperatively toward the ultimate accomplishment of over aching organizational objectives.

The executive, the coach, and other key stakeholders in the organization collaborate to create a partnership to ensure that the executive's learning advances the organization's needs and critical business mandates. The executive coach can be external to the organization or an employee.

The partnership is based on agreed-upon ground rules, time frames, and specific goals and measures of success.

The coaching partnership uses tailored goals and approaches, including

Creation of a development plan
Skill building
Performance improvement
Development for future assignments
Exploration, definition and implementation of the executive's leadership and the organization's business objectives

The coaching process typically involves:

Pre-coaching needs analysis and planning
Contracting
Data gathering
Goal setting and development of coaching plan
Implementation of coaching plan
Measuring and reporting results
Transitioning to long term development

Coaching Models

There are basically two models in coaching. One that allows leaders to change their behaviors, and another model that encourages leaders to change their beliefs and ways of being. Directive coaching, which is sometimes called instructive coaching, generally focuses on changing behaviors. Facilitative coaching can build on changes in behavior to support someone in developing ways of being or it can explore beliefs in order to change behaviors.

Directive or instructive coaching generally focuses on changing a client's behaviors. The coach shows up as an expert in a content or strategy and shares his/her expertise. They might provide resources, make suggestions, model lessons and teach someone how to do something,

Facilitative coaching supports clients to learn new ways of thinking and being through reflection, analysis, observation, and experimentations; this awareness influences their behaviors. The coach does not share expert knowledge, he/she works to build on the client's existing skills, knowledge, and beliefs and helps the client to construct new skills, knowledge, and beliefs that will form the basis for future actions.

Finally, there is transformational coaching which incorporates strategies from directive and facilitative coaching. What makes it distinct is the scope it attempts to affect and the process used.

Transformational coaching is directed at three domains and is intended to affect all three areas:

1. The individual client's behaviors, beliefs, and being
2. The system in which the clients work and
3. The broader social systems in which the clients live.

A transformational coach works to surface the connections between these three domains, to leverage change between them and to intentionally direct the client;s efforts so that the impact he/she has on an individual will reverberate on other levels. Transformational coaching is deeply grounded in systems thinking. Systems thinking is a conceptual framework for seeing interrelationships and patterns of change rather than isolated events. Systems thinking helps us identify the structures that underlie complex situations and discern high and low leverage changes. By seeing wholes, we are much more effective toward transformation.

Transformational coaching directly and intentionally attends to ways of being. We explore language, nonverbal communications, and emotions, and how these affect relationships, performance, and results. As transformational coaches we explore how the client's way of being shifts depending on their contexts. Shifting is natural as he moves into different settings but sometimes the client shifts into ways of being that are not aligned to his vision for organization. A transformational coach helps a client look at these shifts and explore the effects.

Examples of Common Coaching Types

Personal/Life Coaching

The personal/life coach helps individuals gain awareness of and clarify their personal goals and priorities, better understand their thoughts, feelings and options, and take appropriate actions to change their lives, accomplish their goals and feel more fulfilled.

Career Coaching

The career coach helps individuals identify what they want and need from their career, then make decisions and take the needed actions to accomplish their career objectives in balance with the other parts of their lives.

Group Coaching

Group coaches work with individuals in groups. The focus can range from leadership development to career development, stress management to team building. Group coaching combines the benefits of individual coaching with the resources of groups. Individuals learn from each other and the interactions that take place within the group setting.

Performance Coaching

Performance coaches help employees at all levels better understand the requirements of their jobs, the competencies needed to fulfill those requirements, any gaps in their current performance, and opportunities to improve performance. Coaches then work with the employees, their bosses, and others in their workplace to help the employees fill performance gaps and develop plans for further professional development.

Newly Assigned Leader Coaching

Coaches of individuals assigned or hired into new leadership roles help these leaders to "onboard." The goal of the coaching is to clarify with the leader's key constituents the most important responsibilities of his/her new role, his/her deliverables in the first few months of the new assignment, and ways to integrate into the team he/she will lead within the organization. The major focus of this type of coaching is on helping the new leader to assimilate and achieve his/her business objectives.

Relationship Coaching

The relationship coach helps two or more people to form, change, or improve their interactions. The context can be work, personal, or other settings.

High-Potential or Developmental Coaching

The coach works with organizations to develop the potential of individuals who have been identified as key to the organizations' future or are part of the organization's succession plan. The focus of the coaching may include assessment, competency development, or assistance planning and implementing strategic projects.

360 Feedback Coaching

Organizations that use assessment or 360 feedback processes often utilize coaches to help employees interpret the results of their assessments and feedback. In addition, coaches work with individuals to make career decisions and establish professional development plans based on feedback, assessment results and other relevant data.

Targeted Behavioral Coaching

Coaches who provide targeted behavioral coaching help individuals to change specific behaviors or habits or learn new, more effective ways to work and interact with others. This type of coaching often helps individuals who are otherwise very successful in their current jobs or are taking on new responsibilities that require a change in specific behaviors.

Legacy Coaching

The legacy coach helps leaders who are retiring from a key role to decide on the legacy they would like to leave behind. The coach also provides counsel on transitioning out of the leadership role.

Succession Coaching

The succession coach helps assess potential candidates for senior management positions and prepares them for promotion to senior roles. This type of coaching may be used in any organization that is experiencing growth or turnover in its leadership ranks. It is especially helpful in family businesses to maintain the viability of the firm. Since assessment is often part of this intervention, clear expectations and ground rules for confidentiality are essential. It may be necessary in some companies to use separate consultants for assessment and coaching.

Presentation/Communication Skills Coaching

This type of coaching helps individuals gain self-awareness about how they are perceived by others and why they are perceived in that way. Clients learn new ways to interact with others. The use of video recording with feedback allows clients to see themselves as others do. The coach helps clients change the way they communicate and influence others by changing their words, how they say those words, and the body language they use to convey their intended messages.

Team Coaching

One or more team coaches work with the leader and members of a team to establish their team mission, vision, strategy, and rules of engagement with one another. The team leader and members may be coached individually to facilitate team meetings and other interactions, build the effectiveness of the group as a high-performance team and achieve team goals.

COACHING TECHNIQUES

Typically, the coach applies several of the following practices, among others:

Problem solving and planning
Rehearsal role play and on the job practice
Feedback
Dialogue
Clarification or roles, assumptions and priorities
Teaching and applying a variety of management and leadership tools
Referral to other development resources

Building the Partnership

The coaching partnership involves key stakeholders in the coaching process, including:

The executive's manager
Senior management
Human Resources

So, what is different about executive coaching?

As coaching has grown in popularity over the past few years, it is only natural that some authors have tried to differentiate among types of coaching. Some of these categories define coaching type by its goals or ends. Career coaching, for instance, is defined as coaching designed to help an individual make enlightened career choices.

However, the practice of executive coaching may involve many of the types of coaching described below. Thus, an executive coaching engagement may over time touch on the executive's career or personal life issues involving work/life balance, and video feedback is used to work on some particular behavioral or communication problem. However, two factors always distinguish executive coaching from these other types:

1. It always involves a partnership among executive, coach and organization.
2. The individual goals of an executive coaching engagement must always link back and be subordinated to strategic organizational objectives.

Key Principles of Executive Coaching

Executive coaching is one of many approaches or types of interventions that can be used to promote organizational and leadership development. The goal of developing a single leader must always be pursued within the large objective of organizational success. Since executive coaching should be conducted as one of the components of an overall plan for organizational development, executive and coach must both be aware of the larger objectives.

Often the components of the executive coaching process are single, discrete activities in a large organizational development initiative. These components include pre-coaching needs analysis and planning, contracting, data gathering, goal setting, coaching, measuring and reporting results, and transitioning to long term development.

The coach must have enough expertise in organizational dynamics and business management to conduct the coaching with awareness and understanding of the systems issues. Approaching executive coaching from a systems perspective requires the coach to recognize and appreciate the complex organizational dynamics in which the executive operates. The coach ensures a systemic approach through continual awareness of the impact of the coaching process on everyone in the system and vice versa. Accordingly, the coach encourages a shift in the executive's viewpoint, from seeing himself/herself as separate to recognizing his /her interdependence with other people and processes in the organization. This approach encourages respect for the complexity of organizational life and an ability to penetrate beyond this complexity to the underlying structures. In effect, the coach helps the executive to see both the forest and the trees.

Coaching from a systems perspective helps coach and the executive assess developmental needs. By thinking in terms of the big pictures and core issues, both partners will understand long and short term strategies and how all the pieces of the organization fit together into a whole. Systems thinking also encourages all partners to appreciate the impact of the executive's behavioral change on other facets of the organization.

Executive's Commitments

Explore change in vision, values and behaviors.

Examine how your own behaviors and actions affect the systems in which the client operate.

Work in open exploration with the coach and help the coach to understand the forces of the organizational system.

During the coaching process, the client takes responsibility for his/her actions and remains aware of the impact of his/her behavioral changes on others and the organization as a whole.

Coach's Commitments

See the executive, his/her position and the organization through multiple lenses and perspectives.

Maintain an objective and impartial perspective by resisting collusion with the executive or the organization.

Recognize and appreciate the complexity of the organizational structure in which the executive functions.

Encourage the executive to explore both long and short term views.

Recognize the interaction of all parts in the whole-especially how change in one of the executive's behaviors may affect other behaviors and other people.

Help the executive distinguish between high and low leverage changes. Encourage commitment to the highest leverage action to achieve results.

Other Partners' Commitments

Identify and share organizational information that may help the coach and the executive recognize and understand the context, organizational forces, business-related issues, and financial constraints they must factor into the coaching.

Guide the coach regarding organizational changes that may influence the coaching.

Be willing to examine and possibly change aspects of the organizational system in order to improve both the executive's and the organization's performance.

Executive Coaching Is About Adult Development

Since coaching is a learning process that leads to behavioral change, a person may have to unlearn old, less productive ways of thinking and doing, and replace those behaviors with more effective ones. A coach needs to understand incorporate the principles of adult learning into his approach.

Principles of Adult Learning

New information, ideas and material need to be grounded in the familiar. New information must be related to the person's existing framework of experience and beliefs.

More than anywhere else, new learning in a business setting must be applied to the individual's situation. In other words, it must have purpose and be practical.

New learning must be reinforced with a variety of approaches. Different people learn best in different ways. Some techniques include role-playing and rehearsal, reading books and articles, completing selective exercises, writing in a journal and participating in one-on-one discussion.

Learning and Change

Learning is really about change ... change in attitude, perception or behavior. Thus, it requires:

Feedback about one's self and how one is seen or experienced by other.

Awareness of the need to change and accepting responsibility to change.

Identification of the most critical development needs.

Focused goal setting and action planning to design realistic strategies for enhancing the individual's effectiveness.

Linkage of action plans to the individual's real world situation.

Experimentation with new behavior or approaches.

Knowledge of how success is measured and acknowledgment when it occurs.

Implementation of the plans in the work situation.

Seek advice, counsel and help from others.

- Ongoing follow-up to ensure new behavior is internalized.

Executive Coaching a unique approach for results

What makes a good executive coach an effective and successful coach? You ask 10 people and you will get 10 different answers. But, whatever approach is used, it must achieve measurable and lasting results.

As a psychologist i was trained and influenced by a world renowned clinical psychologist by the name of Dr. Arnold A. Lazarus. He was a significant contributor to the evolution of psychology through the integration of a cognitive behavioral approach called Multimodal therapy. It involved an integration of a variety of techniques to identify causes of emotional or psychological issues and in a systematic way, identifies ways of validating causes and implementing well proven strategies or techniques to obtain changes and positive results.

In his book **Multimodal Behavior Therapy** (1976), Dr. Lazarus said, "Many therapists waste time... They tend to ask irrelevant questions and apply techniques of dubious validity. A multimodal orientation presupposes no identification with any specific school of psychological thought. Its practitioners are pragmatists who enforce scientific empiricism and logical positivism without succumbing to unnecessary redundant reasoning. Conceptually, the positivist position is taken in combination with the stance of a creative synthesist. The multi-modal therapists focus their approach on learning principles and more especially, social learning, cognitive processes and behavioral principles for which there is experimental evidence."

Dr Lazarus indicated that. "...Our primary assumption is that the more people learn in therapy, the broader their coping responses become, the less likely are they to relapse." Furthermore, he states that "the modalities of behavior, are spread over behavior, affect, sensation, imagery, cognition and interpersonal processes." These six modalities may be said to constitute human "personality."

While in the field of psychology, the attention is on feelings and emotions in the area of executive coaching the goal is on changing behaviors. The goal is to focus not on what a client feels about a situation but how he or she acts in a given situation. In my coaching I have utilized many of the multimodal principles, which have been successful in cognitive behavioral psychotherapy, and applied them in a non-clinical way to help clients become aware of behaviors and to gain insights about options or changes to their behaviors. I have spent the past fifteen years successfully applying the principles and using these strategies to help clients make measurable and permanent behavioral changes.

Key Skills for Executive Coaching

Coaching involves a number of well-developed skills. The active practice of these key skills can make the consultant more effective as an executive coach.

The following are important for effective executive coaching.

Active Listening
Focused Questioning
Using assessment tools and in-depth interviews
Creating new approaches and developing a plan
Providing candid, supportive feedback
Organizational understanding

Examples of these strategies include:

Active Listening

Summarize what you have heard the person say. Paraphrasing helps to confirm that you understand what the client meant to communicate. As you listen, try to do the following:

Stay fully in the moment and stay focused on the client.
Listen for specific information or an opening to ask questions to further clarification.
Observe, interpret and analyze as you go. Ask yourself: What patterns are emerging?

What is missing? What doesn't fit? Be prepared to create something from what you hear rather than just take in information.

Focused Questioning

The use of questioning and probing in the coaching process in invaluable. Typically, you would start with broad questions and gradually move to more specific ones to get at the client's issues. A good rule of thumb in questioning is to move from the simple to the complex. In short, try these methods:

Identify what the client does well and acknowledge these behaviors as valuable.

Re-frame, clarify, verify and amplify information the client presents.

Get beneath the surface to the underlying issues.

Ask questions in such a way that you lead the clients to discover things themselves rather than giving them information.

Using assessment tools and in-depth interviews. A well-developed interview is the key to obtaining a full picture of the organizational climate, the perceptions of the client's superiors and others, and the client's own view of himself.

Creating New Approaches and Developing a Plan

Helping the client see the gap that exists between where they are and where they want to be at the end of the process is essential. Using specific measurable goals and timelines make the plan achievable.

Be imaginative and look for a variety of solutions.

Break down plans to manageable, small steps, set micro-goals, move from easy to more difficult.

Move between the big picture, and the small details; help the client to see the connections between them.

Make the plan realistic for the individual, the organization and the culture while taking into consideration any restraints in the situation.

Move forward without controlling the outcome.

Monitoring the process and keeping it moving forward is critical, but focus on shared responsibility and accountability to ensure that the process made is owned by your client, not just you.

Be agile and ready to go where the client needs you to. Be sure to honor what they need to work on, and keep them focused on the action and development plan outcomes.

Use breakdowns or backslides as material to work with. Change is not always linear or smooth and sometimes what you think is the right approach is not. Your client will often surprise you when you think you have the answers.

Providing Candid, Supportive Feedback

While a coach will always have the responsibility to provide observation and feedback, using various approaches and supportive techniques can better ensure success and real change.

Speak to what is happening in the moment.

Keep comments specific and timely to enable the client to handle them more easily.

Challenge client's assumptions, offer alternate views, make distinctions or clarify meanings.

Provide a new perspective by placing situations or events in larger context.

Be vigilant. Point out behaviors that is not consistent with stated values and goals.

Confront old habits and patterns; offer new ways to act an to reframe situation.

State the truth as you see it, however stay neutral. Present your comments as information to be considered by the client.

Encourage and support engine efforts to change, not just those that are successful.

Always check with the client to make sure that feedback is understood and that the client is feeling supported in the process, even if the feedback is uncomfortable.

Ask, Don't Tell

Guide the conversation with questions and listen for the answers.

Ask questions that initiate dialogue.
Clarify information is accurate.
Draw out the information already inside the person.

It is amazing what you can learn if you ask a question and then quietly wait for the answer. Guide the discussion. Do not assume you need to provide the answers. Balance good questions with good listening. This respectful approach often produces more trust, more information and sometimes answers to questions you have not yet asked.

Ways to use this technique include:

Ask questions that encourage dialogue.

What outcomes are you hoping to achieve?
How will things look different if you make this change?
What's worked well for you in the past?

Draw out the information your coaching partner has not yet mentioned.

Can you describe the situation as you see it?

What do you think caused you to react this way?

What do you imagine could get in the way of your success?

Provide the direction, not the answers.

What is the most important thing you have learned from this situation?

Based on the conversation we have just had, what do you see as you options for handling the situation?

How might you handle this situation in the future?

Reframing the Picture

Encourage the discovery of different perspectives.

Create an awareness of multiple perspectives.

Use metaphors to modify or clarify interpretations.

Encourage more strategic and long term views.

There are many ways to view the same set of circumstances, including from another person's point of view. Reframing affords the opportunity to see a situation from a different or new--and perhaps more realistic--perspective. It can also help to uncover blind spots or missing points. Sometimes a more global or balanced view of things provides powerful motivation for changing behavior.

Some examples of this technique include:

Create an awareness of multiple perspectives.

If you were the other person, how would you want it handled?

It is interesting you saw it that way. Can I tell you what it looks like to me?

If Mr. X was there, how would he describe the situation?

How about Ms. X? How would she describe it?

Use metaphors to modify or clarify interpretations.

It sounds like she's tilling the soil and planting seeds when he thinks it's harvest time. If you were standing on a hilltop looking down, what would the situation look like to you?

If you were the ship's captain, how would you chart the course?

Encourage more strategic and long-term views:

Two years from now, when people look back at this project, what will they say about its effects on the organization?

What implications does this plan have for other departments? What effects are likely to occur in the organization as a whole?

Can you see how you handled the situation differently than you would have two months ago?

In-The-Moment Feedback

Give spontaneous feedback that builds trust, support and open communication.

Point out behavior when it happens

Invite your coaching partner to examine behavior

Connect the current behavior to the impact it may have

Give feedback on behavior involves courage and respect. Be direct in reflecting back your observations and assumptions about what you are hearing or seeing in the moment and the impact. You need to keep collaboration effective and the learning process ongoing. Your immediate comments on behaviors observed in coaching sessions can be relevant to larger workplace issues.

Here are some ways to use this strategy:

Point out behavior when it happens:

> May I comment on what I am observing at the moment and see if I have got it straight?
> I think I might be hearing a contradiction here. Can we talk about it?
> Can we pause for a moment? May I react to what you just said?
> Invite your coaching partner to examine a behavior.
> This might be just my own personal reaction but let me tell you how it makes me feel.
> It seemed to me that your tone of voice was a little harsh just now, even though your words were not. Can we talk about this?
> Three different topics we discussed today evoked the same response from you. What is the common theme?

Connect the current behavior to the impact it may have:

> What effect do you think your response might have on others?
> I wonder if you ever use the same body language and tone of voice in business meetings?
> How do you think your reaction to that topic would affect your subordinates at work?

Guided Learning

Start with the premise of not knowing the answers and learn by experimentation.

> Challenge the need to have all the answers
> Foster an attitude of learning and risk-taking
> Encourage your partner to experiment with new behaviors

It is precisely those areas where you or your coaching partner do not know the answers that the most productive learning can occur.

The first step is having the openness to say, "I do not know" and to adopt the attitude of a learner. Then you and your partner an experiment with the new behaviors to find out what works best. As always, the selected behaviors are those most closely linked to organizational goals.

Some ways to use this technique include:

Challenge the need to have all the answers.

> It is ok not to know the answer. Sometimes that is the best starting point.
> There really is not any one right solution. Sometimes I find it works best just to play around with different options.
> You have said that your past approach has not worked very well. I am wondering if it is time to try something new.

Foster an attitude of learning and risk-taking.

How do you learn best? Let's apply some of those approaches to this situation. Setting aside the risks for the moment, is there a radical, outside-of-the-box solution that might work?

Think of the person you admire most in the company. What would that person be likely to do in this situation?

Encourage your partner to experiment with new behaviors.

What have you tried? What else could you try?

Is there a completely different way for you to respond to that situation?

How and when might you test out some of these new behaviors?

Promote Partnerships

Assist your coaching partner in building mutually beneficial relationships:

Explore the benefits of partnership behaviors

Use the coaching relationship to model partnership behaviors. Encourage the creation of many partnerships. Sometimes exceptional performers are overly self-reliant. Taking a partnership approach to organizational relationships builds advocates and supporters, fosters team development and generally increases productivity. The coaching relationship offers an opportunity to create successful partnerships and yes, their effects. Sometimes the first step is as simple as offering assistance or making a request.

Examples of how to use this strategy include:

Explore the benefits of partnership behaviors.

What do you look for in a partner?

What could be gained by partnering with that person?

If you initiated a partnership, what would you offer that person?

Use the coaching relationship to model partnership behaviors.

What is working well in our partnership?

How can you apply the way we interact as partners to other relationships you might want to develop?

Can you think of someone with whom you have had little interaction who you would want to give feedback or coaching to?

Encourage the creation of many partnerships.

Who might you ask to work with you on this project? If there someone you would like to build a more effective working relationship with?

What are you doing right now that might be improved upon or accelerated by new partners elsewhere in your organization?

Is there anyone you have never teamed up with who might benefit from you expertise?

Straight Talk

Tell your coaching partner the things that no one else is willing to mention.

Be sensitive to the possible emotional impact.

Be objective and non-judgmental in your presentation.

Use specific examples.

There are times when it is better to stop listening and offer some very direct comments. Providing a realistic view of the facts you have observed about situations and about your partner's behavior is an essential part of productive coaching. Sometimes challenging your partner can help the person move to a higher level of performance. Be sensitive and respectful when you use this high-impact approach.

Some examples of how to use this strategy include:

Be sensitive to the possible emotional impact.

> Is it ok to tell you something that I think might be very useful, but could make you uncomfortable?
>
> I would like to give you some information based on my observations. I would like you not to react immediately, but to take some time to reflect on it before we discuss it. Would you be willing to do that?
>
> May I give you some feedback and trust you will take it in the way it is intended: As a way to help you move forward?

Be objective and nonjudgmental in your presentation.

> At times, all of us engage in behaviors that do not produce the results we desire.
>
> Sometimes people react automatically to certain situations.
>
> Learning new behavior can sometimes be difficult.

Use specific examples.

> I have received feedback from several people who have all pointed to the same pattern of behavior in similar circumstances.

If you made that comment to your boss in the same way you just said it to me, it might produce some undesirable results.

This behavior is similar to one mentioned in your 360 feedback.

Behavior

Behavioral-rehearsal. With this technique, your coaching partner is given instructions and sets up what it would be like to deal with a difficult situation, for example, dealing with a difficult client. By rehearing various outcomes, your partner gains insights and awareness of how to behave regardless of how difficult the client.

Modeling/ Positive reinforcement. Using this strategy, your coaching partner is able to watch and model, through discussion, films or observing other managers so he/she has examples of how to behave. Then, with input from the executive coach, he/she gains positive reinforcement when her behavior is appropriate for a situation. For example, being polite and professional in the presence of an abusive client

Self-Monitoring. This strategy gives your partner tools to be aware of his /her behavior in a given situation, and he/she can monitor and make adjustments as appropriate. This is a good situation where emotional intelligence is used and understood by your coaching partner so he/she is aware of his/her behaviors and can adjust such behaviors so as to remain in control of his/her emotions and be professional, even when the potential to become upset, angry or out of control emotionally exists.

Imagery

Goal rehearsal. With this behavior, your coaching partner sets what the outcome looks like and can rehearse, via imagery or role play so he/she can visualize the outcome and gain awareness of what situations will cause him/her not to meet the desired outcome. For example, losing control when dealing with a difficult client and getting sarcastic. A better outcome would include redirecting his/her behavior, visualizing himself/herself staying in control and getting a sense of what it feels like to be in control so his/her behaviors will follow the imagery.

Positive imagery. This is an extension of goal rehearsal. With this strategy, your partner can visualize the outcome of what it feels like to remain positive and have his/her boss give her praise for dealing successfully with a difficult client and remaining in control or reducing the client's anger.

Empty chair. This is a favorite strategy used in coaching and therapy. Here, your coaching partner talks to a person, as if he/her were in the chair and can define what he/she wants to say and rehearse it while remaining in control of his/her feelings. The goal to be achieved is that as your partner rehearses and practices the points he/she wants to make, then when the real situation occurs, your partner will know what behaviors to exhibit and will remain focused on achieving the desired outcome and remain calm.

Affect

Anger-expression. With this strategy, the coach prompts the coaching partner to verbalize what he/she is feeling, clarify the situation and help the partner stay focused, be in control and redirect any negative energy or emotions into positive behaviors.

Anxiety-management training. Here the coach helps the coaching partner explore issues or roadblocks to achieving a certain outcome in behavior and helps him/her to reduce his/her anxiety and learn how to handle the difficult client or boss and no longer be anxious but rather working to meet the needs of the boss or client while disarming their anger.

Sensation

Mediation. By teaching the coaching partner to take a breath, to relax and to stay calm, he/she will not be controlled by fear or emotions but rather to act out of a state calmness.

Focusing. This strategy helps the client to stay alert and using the role-play or empty chair exercises combined with being focused helps the partner stay positive, use his/her energy in such a way as to be in control and be alert to client behaviors and how to adjust his/her behavior so as to achieve the desired outcome.

Cognition

Reading material. Using various readings and homework assignments between sessions, the coaching partner is given information to help him/her learn to master a particular point. This reading material is used as a springboard for continued learning, and discussions during coaching sessions are used to teach and help your partner learn to develop more tools to use in doing her job.

Problem solving. A very pragmatic strategy is that the coach working with the coaching partner addresses any number of issues. Through the use of Socratic questions, the coach helps the partner define the problem, develop potential solutions and implement, via trial and error, various solutions that will help him/her manage a given situation.

Self instruction. This strategy enables the partner to be aware of certain behaviors, and based on his/her training, reading and personal development will be able to change behaviors as he/she talks to himself/herself and instructs himself/herself, in a positive way, what the desired behavioral outcome should be.

Interpersonal

Communication training. A list of ongoing instructions and awareness training that the coach provides to your coaching partner. Typically, it includes training on how to become a better communicator, listener and presenter. This is the key to establishing and maintaining an effective interaction with his/her team.

Social skills and assertive training. One of the most important skills that the coach frequently provides to your partner is awareness of appropriate social interaction skills, such as how to politely but firmly make a point to a team member, boss or subordinate in a way that does not alienate the party but informs. The coach also helps the partner became more polished in his/her presentations and how to read social cues so he /she is aware of the body language and social cues being given as he/she interacts with the team.

The effectiveness of a good executive coaching program is based on building a trusting and open relationship with the client. Being honest, respectful and over the first few sessions, having the client know the coach is dedicated to your coaching partner's success. The coach is viewed as a supporter and catalyst to help the your partner make positive change, without controlling, intimidating or creating negative experiences.

There are many ways a client becomes aware or gains insight about his or her behavior. However, my approach allows for a systematic assessment, building a trusting business relationship and using the above cognitive behavioral strategies to empower the client to gain insights, learn new ways of behaving and learns to mastery the ways to act so as to self regulate his/her behavior and establish measurable changes that are permanent and help him or her to maintain such changes.

ADDENDUM

Suggested Introduction Sentences

Active Listening

well…

how would you phrase it…

what I am hearing, then…

if I were to clarify what you said….

I understand you are saying…is that right?

you are saying many things…let's try to clarify what you mean

I hear you say…what are you feeling about that?

Clarifying important points

do I understanding that you mean…

tell me more…

can you think of an example...

what do you really mean...?

when you say...what do you mean

so is that thought different or similar to...

I am intriqued by that statement, tell me more...

I am interested by that last statement, can you clarify...

what strikes my fancy is when you said ...

I wonder...

Nonjudgmental statements

when you said... the participant seems pleased...

can you identify why the project went well?

so, how would you define what made the lesson successful...

Probing questions

can you describe another way to ...?

tell me a different way that you could say or do...?

so if you did that action, what would be the outcome?

is that action similar or different that other actions you have taken?

what is another way you might…?

what was effect on your audience…?

can you define the actions that made this a success?

in the past have you done anything similar to get the same result?

describe what made this a success?

how did you reach that decision?

Faciliative Questions

Cathartic quesitons

it appears to me that you are very emotional about…can we explore what might be behind those feeling?

what are you feeling at this moment? what do you think is behind those feeling?

if I did that I might also have those strong emotions, can you describe them and what would give you a different outcome

Catalytic Questions

in the past have you had smiliar outcomes? how you would label them?

it is difficult for me to understand you when you… can you help me know where you are coming from?

if you did it differently, how would it change and would you have a similar outcome?

in the last 10 minutes you have spoken about many things and the last thing you said was....really what are you feeling and what do you mean?

Supportive Questions

it is obvious to me that when you....the team was.....what do you think was happening?

you have many ideas and they all seem good...which one do you think will be the best?

if you were to identify why the program was successful what would be those points?

you have many useful suggestions...can you tell me more about...

I am inspired by your enthusiam and persistence...are you aware of all that energy?.

the team felt you did a great job when you...

do you feel confident that you efforts will be successful

Directive Questions

Confrontation questions

are you open to exploring what you meant when you said?

ae you willing to discuss the reasons behind your statements?

I am interested to understand what you mean and how you feel about...

if you did it differently, what would that look like...?

so give me a different way in which you would...?

so, if you did that...what would it look like and would you get the same result?

can you describe a different way of doing it ?

can you imagine what it woul look like if you did it this way?

you appear to be very emotional what is going on?

I have noticed some good result...what did you do to make this happen?

Informative Questions

I recently read a book by... and he/she made some excellent points about...

have you considered using this strategy...to achieve your desired outcome?

I will introduce you to...and he/she may be helpful....

I have suggested that you supervisor discuss...with you

Prescriptive Questions

with you permission, I would like to discuss this matter with your boss

do you understand what the policy is about...can you tell me so I am enlightened?

last week you stated that you would do...what is the status of your efforts?

if you are open and willing I would love to share some experience I have had dealing with...

have you tried....I think it may be helpful.